Mercedes de la Garza

THE MAYAS
3000 YEARS OF CIVILIZATION

194 Colour illustrations

MONCLEM
EDICIONES

BONECHI

CONTENTS

INTRODUCTION

The Mayas, inhabiting a vast, rich region of America, created one of the most original and grandiose civilizations ever known. They are not a homogeneous group but rather a collection of groups with different languages, customs and historical background yet at the same time sharing traits that allow them to be classed as a single cultural unit. In turn this unit is itself part of a larger one — Mesoamerican culture — that in pre-Hispanic times covered central and southern Mexico and Central America. The Olmecs, Nahuas, Zapotecs, Mixtecs, Totonacs, Tarascans and others belonged to this culture.

The Maya, or Mayance, groups are mainly distinguished by their languages, belonging to a large linguistic family that grew from an original tongue spoken in western Guatemala in the third millennium B.C. These languages (not to be considered as dialects, since each one has a structured grammar) number some 28, the most important being Yucatec Maya, Chontal, Tzeltal, Tzotzil, Tojolabal, Lacandon, Kanjobal, Chuj, Quiche, Cakchiquel, Kekchi, Pokomam and Pokomchi.

The historical development of the pre-Hispanic Maya civilization is divided into three broad periods:

The Pre-Classic, when the distinguishing features of the Maya culture took shape; agriculture becomes the basis of economy, the first villages and ceremonial centers are built, and various cultural activities grow up around religion.

The Classic, beginning around the third century, was a period when all fields flourished: great strides are made in agriculture, technology and trade; political, social, priestly and military hierarchies are consolidated; great ceremonial centers and cities are built where science, arts and the recording of history flourish.

Around the 9th century sees the collapse of culture, perhaps because of an economic, and consequently socio-political, crisis. Political and cultural activities come to an end in the great Classic cities in the Central area. Many of them are abandoned, marking the beginning of the **Post-Classic.**

In contrast to the Central area, where Maya culture was never to flourish again, the Northern and Southern areas experienced a cultural revival under the influence of groups arriving mainly from the Central Plateau. The Northern area boasts the imposing site of Chichén Itzá with its remarkable Toltec influenced works of art; the city of Mayapán is founded which seems to have politically dominated all the other centers in the region. In 1441 a war broke out that destroyed Mayapán; the main cities on the Yucatan Peninsula were abandoned and new urban centers arose. Meanwhile, great cities such as Gumarcah in Guatemala are built in the Southern area.

From this time until the arrival of the Spanish, practical and military interests override religious, intellectual and artistic creation; many cultural features are secularized (i.e. they lose their religious character) and Maya history takes a different course, as war and trade become the predominant activities. Powerful military states develop, such as the one created by the Quiche in the Guatemala highlands and trading empires like those founded by the Chontal and Putun groups on the Gulf of Mexico.

The **Post-Classic** period ends with the Spanish Conquest. This put an end to the development of Mesoamerican culture; the Mayas were overcome and confined on their own territory.

Reference is often made to the «disappearance» of the Mayas, but this is a mistake: what really disappeared was its freedom and the imposing culture created in pre-Hispanic times. Mayas, with their everyday customs and most of their religious beliefs still intact keep to their original regions, upholding their ancestors' concept of life and the world.

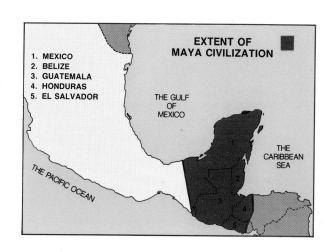

1. MEXICO
2. BELIZE
3. GUATEMALA
4. HONDURAS
5. EL SALVADOR

EXTENT OF MAYA CIVILIZATION

THE GULF OF MEXICO

THE CARIBBEAN SEA

THE PACIFIC OCEAN

Left. An example of the realism achieved by the Mayas of Palenque, Chiapas, Mexico. A stucco portrait from the Classic period.

In the Highlands of the Southern area, peaks rise to 4000 meters, such as the Agua and Fuego volcanoes towering over Lake Atitlán, Guatemala.

GEOGRAPHY OF THE AREA

Mayance groups settled in an area of nearly 400,000 square kilometers that includes the present-day states of Yucatan, Campeche, Quintana Roo and eastern Tabasco and Chiapas in Mexico; and Guatemala, Belize and western parts of El Salvador and Honduras in Central America.

It is a region of wide geographical contrasts. In terms of relief it is divided into Highlands and Lowlands, and in terms of artistic and cultural characteristics, into Southern, Central and Northern areas.

Southern Area

This area includes the Pacific coast, the Highlands of Guatemala, part of El Salvador and part of Chiapas. The climate is mild in summer, with a period of heavy rainfall, and cold and dry in winter, but torrid on the coastal plain. The Highlands are made up of volcanic mountains covered in forests of conifers and other cold-climate trees. This is where the Motagua and Usumacinta rivers rise, the first emptying into the Gulf of Honduras and the second into the Gulf of Mexico after flowing through Tabasco and Chiapas. The highest points

Some of the animals with an important role in everyday Maya life and religion were deer, jaguars, macaws and wild turkeys.

The Agua Azul falls in Chiapas, famous for their beautiful color, are on the Tulijá river, one of the many water courses flowing down from the mountains to the valley of Tabasco.

in Guatemala are the Sierra Cuchumatanes and the three volcanoes Atitlán, Agua and Fuego, which rise to almost 4000 meters. In Chiapas is the Sierra Madre, which changes its name to the Sierra de Soconusco in the southeast, with the Tacana volcano of over 4000 meters.

There are several lakes of volcanic origin in Guatemala, such as Amatitlán, Atitlán and Izabal, which is linked to the Gulf of Honduras.

Central Area

This is the largest of the Maya areas, covering the Department of Peten in Guatemala; parts of Honduras and Chiapas; Belize, Tabasco and the southern part of the Yucatan Peninsula. The average height of the area is 300 meters, though in Belize the Maya Mountains rise as high as 1000 meters.

The climate of this region is hot and humid with year round rainfall of over 400 cm. Several rivers flow through it, e.g. the Pasion and Candelaria, but the greatest is the Grijalva, which after rising in the mountains of Chiapas and Guatemala flows through the impressive Sumidero Canyon to empty into the Gulf of Mexico. The largest lake is Peten Itza.

The area is covered by tropical rain forest containing a very wide variety of tree species. Some of these, such as the mahogany, sapodilla and kapok grow to as high as 30-40 meters.

Northern Area

This area covers the northern half of the Yucatan Peninsula. It is a flat expanse, except for the Sierra, or Puuc, a chain of hills about 200 meters high stretching from Campeche to Yucatan. The climate is tropical, with summer rains and a steppe-like dry season; rainfall is scanty, not even reaching 50 cm. per year.

There are only three, very short rivers here: Champoton, Hondo and Lagartos, and one lake - Bacalar. However, because the subsoil is limestone there are several types of underground water deposits. The most remarkable of these are the «cenotes» (*dzonot* in Maya) that are formed when the roofs of caves collapse. Cenotes have always played an important role in the settlement of the area, as they are the main source of water.

Vegetation in the Northern Area is forest and scrub and, like in the other two areas is rich in medicinal herbs, including hallucinogenic plants and fungi.

Left. Yaxchilán («Green Stones») one of the most striking cities in the Usumacinta style, standing on the banks of the river and surrounded by the Chiapas rain forest, flourished in the Late Classic.

Above. Sisal, a source of a tough fiber, was little used in pre-Hispanic times, but was grown and utilized extensively in the 19th. and early 20th. centuries.

Cenote in the forest of the Central area, formed in a limestone surface similar to Yucatan's.

The Caribbean coast and a Maya watchtower on Ak cove, Quintana Roo, Mexico.

Right. The Olmecs produced massive sculptures, such as this Pre-Classic priest's head, in stone brought from up to 100km. away.

CULTURAL INFLUENCES

Right from the beginning of their history the Mayas had links with other Mesoamerican cultures and were influenced by them. During the pre-Classic period the Gulf Cost saw the rise of one of the most remarkable of pre-Hispanic cultures: the *Olmecs*. Between 1200 and 900 B.C. they created the first great Mesoamerican state (perhaps theocratic) while others were still defining themselves.

The Olmecs built the first pyramid in Mesoamerica, at La Venta, and carved huge, monolithic heads, altars and other striking works. Olmec art, which also includes numerous works in jade and other materials, is one of the most perfect in the pre-Columbian world.

The Olmecs seem to have sown the seeds of writing — later developed by the Mayas — while their religion was centered on serpents and jaguars, the two animals that

symbolized Mesoamerica. This culture influenced other contemporary Mesoamerican groups, especially between 800 and 400 B.C.

In the Southern Maya area Olmec influence fused with local cultures, giving rise to another great culture known as «Izapa» that lasted from 600 B.C. to 150 A.D. Many sites were established in this region, but the most important are Kaminaljuyu in Guatemala and Izapa in Chiapas.

In Izapa stelae were erected along with altars carved with narrative and ritual scenes that are the direct ancestors of Maya art and of the main religious beliefs.

At the beginning of the Christian era another great culture made its appearance in the Valley of Mexico: Teotihuacán.

The Teotihuacán people created the first great city in Mesoamerica, one that contained up to 85,000 inhabitants between 500 and 600 A.D. Teotihuacán culture

Altar 5 at La Venta, Tabasco, Mexico. A priest holds a dead child with strange facial markings, perhaps changed by sacrifice to the gods. Pre-Classic period.

Jadeite mask with a jaguar-like mouth; an example of Olmec stone carving from Tres Zapotes, Veracruz, Mexico. Pre-Classic period.

is expressed mainly in a severe style of architecture and highly artistic painting and pottery. These people had a certain knowledge of the calendar, astronomy and mathematics, as well as a polytheistic religion including gods that the later Nahuas would worship. Thanks to their highly developed trade network they wielded considerable influence on all Mesoamerica, shown in the Maya area by pottery and some features of architecture and sculpture. These are evident in Central area cities such as Tikal during the Classic period.

Later, when the Maya state collapsed in the Central area the North and South came under the influence of groups

In the Early pre-Classic the first great Mesoamerican city, Teotihuacán on the Central Plateau of Mexico, became a cultural center that spread its influence everywhere.

The city of Tula, Hidalgo, flourished after the fall of Teotihuacan. The warrior-priests of these sculptures conquered Chichén Itza around 1000 A.D.

arriving from the Central Plateau, particularly the Nahuas known as «Toltecs». These brought their religion centered on Quetzalcoatl and also the architectural style of their major city, Tula, (now in the state of Hidalgo), which would be revitalized in the city of Chichén Itzá. In the Southern area the influence of these groups shows in texts written by the Mayas after the Conquest such as the Quiche «Popol Vuh». Other Nahua groups arrived in the Maya area towards the end of the post-Classic era to influence living and cultural patterns in the North and South: Aztecs, who created a wide empire dominating almost all other Mesoamerican cultures.

Left. Maya social and political stratification. Top to bottom: Halach uinic, *the supreme governor;* Batabes, *governors of dependent cities; nobles and warriors, craftsmen, and finally peasant-farmers.*

Classic period clay figurine from Jaina, Campeche, Mexico, of a nobleman wearing jewelry and a sophisticated headdress.

Below. Figure from a door post in the Temple of the Cross, Palenque, Mexico (Late Classic) with the features of the god Bolon D'zacab. The jaguar skin and tobacco identify him as a shaman.

SOCIAL ORGANIZATION

When agriculture began (in the lower pre-Classic phase) and Maya groups became sedentary this was the base of their economy, supplemented by hunting, fishing and food collecting. Their farming system was based on «slash and burn», i.e. felling trees and undergrowth, burning them and then sowing with the help of a pointed digging stick at the beginning of the rainy season. Social organization at this time continued to be tribal: family related groups sharing one culture, one language and one territory. The economy was very basic, founded on family needs, but gradually a division grew that finally resulted in a class differentiation.

As agriculture became more sophisticated, with irrigation systems and the cultivation of commercial crops such as cacao and cotton, population increased and ceremonial centers were built. At the same time social rank became more clearly defined, leading to a division of labor.

The theocratically governed ceremonial centers and cities that multiplied during the Classic period were inhabited by members of the ruling class. They devoted themselves to intellectual pursuits such as social and economic planning, public works, political organization, scientific studies (mathematics, astronomy, chronology, medicine) and to

Detail from Stele 1 at Bonampak (Classic period) illustrating skull deformation and also the hairstyle and ear plugs of Maya lords. A glyph appears in front of the nose.

Figurine from Jaina, classical period, representing an elder nobleman with a long tunic and a war shield.

Facing page. Above left. Figurine from the island of Jaina showing a common Maya bodily adornment: scarification. Color was first applied to the skin and then designs were cut in.

Facing page. Above right. Stone lintel from the Temple of the Frescoes, Bonampak, Chiapas, showing a war scene. Classic period.

Facing page. Below left. Part of a copy in the National Museum of Anthropology, Mexico City, of a fresco from Bonampak showing a procession of musicians. Classic period.

recording the history of noble lineages with a highly developed system of writing. Specialist workers (builders, artists and craftsmen), as well as servants, also lived in the cities, while the farming population lived outside, near the fields. Trade was on a large scale, and merchants made up another separate social class.

Although there were many changes at the end of the Classic period and in the post-Classic, including the predominance of State and military interests, social stratification remained firm. The only modification seems to have been a division of the supreme power into political and religious aspects, which before were vested in a single person. The highest social class consisted of lords or nobles, called *almehenoob* by the Yucate-

Lintel 53 from Yaxchilán, dated 766 A.D. (Classic period). The Halach uinic holds a «mannikin scepter» and is receiving the accoutrements of a shaman from the hands of a woman.

can Mayas, people of noble lineage destined by divine right to rule over the others, through either political or religious power or by force. Governors (headed by the *Halach uinic*, the «True man»), priests (a class headed by the *Ahau can*, «Lord Serpent») war leaders and perhaps merchants, who had certain political roles, belonged to this privileged class.

Below them were the «commoners», people without noble lineage, called *ah chembal uinicoob*, «inferior men» — builders, artists, craftsmen and farmers. There were also slaves (*pentacoob*), who were criminals, prisoners of war, orphans or the children of slaves, but these were not numerous and did not play an important part in production like they did in the Old World The materially productive class was that of the *ah chembal uinicoob*, which enabled nobles to be productive intellectually, i.e. to foster religion, science and art. Thus, the imposing works of art, the hundreds of hieroglyphic texts and all the other remains of the pre-Hispanic Maya world are also lasting tribute to these «inferior men».

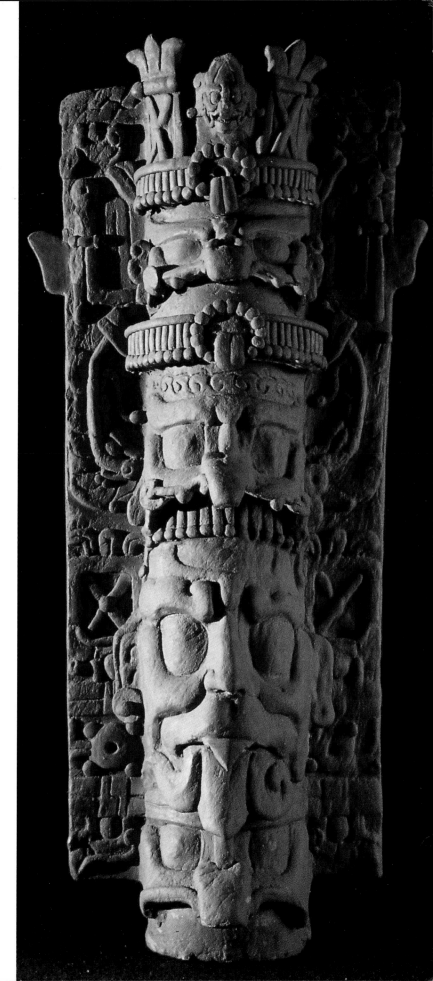

Large clay incense burner from Palenque, Chiapas, of the Sun god Kinich Ahau with a headdress of tiered masks. Classic period.

RELIGION

All Maya cultural creations are based on a religious concept of the world, since the world itself was held to be of divine origin and pervaded by sacred forces that determined everything that happened. These forces were the gods, embodied in natural phenomena such as the stars and the rain (*Chaac*); they were also the forces of death, such as the gods that brought disease and even death itself. But these deities also had animal forms: the Sun is sometimes a macaw or a jaguar; rain is a snake; death, a bat or an owl, etc. In plastic art they are portrayed as fantastic beings, a mixture of several animals, or human shapes with some animal or plant feature such as a snake's eyes, talons, fangs and leaves sprouting from the forehead.

The universe was made up of three great horizontal planes: the heavens, the earth and the underworld. The heavens, divided into thirteen levels, were inhabited by the stars, which are deities, such as the Moon (*Ixchel*) and Venus (*Nohok Ek*). The Sky was identified with the god *Itzamná*, «*dragon*», often shown as a two-headed, feathered snake or as a dragon (a mixture of snake, bird, lizard and deer). He, the supreme god in the Maya pantheon, symbolized the fertilizing powers of the cosmos that gave life to the whole universe.

The Earth was envisaged as a flat expanse floating on water, but also as a large crocodile or alligator with plants growing out of its back. Yucatecan Mayas called it *Chac Mumul Ain*, «The Great Muddy Crocodile».

The underworld was divided into nine levels. In the lowest of these lived the god of Death *Ah Puch*, «The Fleshless One», otherwise known as *Kisin*, «The Stinking One», and portrayed as a skeleton or a rotting human body.

The three levels were in turn divided hor-

The Sacred Well of Chichén Itzá, Yucatan. This made the city a center of pilgrimage ever since the Classic period as it was believed to be the home of the Rain god.

The god Itzamná in the shape of a dragon spouting water from his jaws. Below, the goddess Ixchebel Yax, emptying a pitcher and a black god of war. From p.74 of the Dresden Codex.

Above right. The caves of Balancanche, Yucatan, Mexico. In pre-Hispanic times these were the sanctuary of the Rain god. A great «tree» of a joined stalagmite and stalactite standing in a pool of water is surrounded by incense burners with the image of the god Tlaloc from the Central Plateau.

Right below. Ah Puch, god of Death, carrying an ax, portrayed behind a sacred calendar. Madrid Codex, page 16.

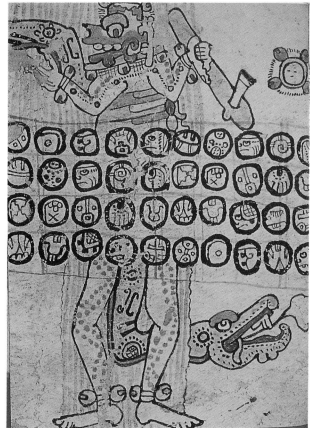

izontally into four sections or «paths» coinciding with the four cardinal points. Each of these had a color assigned to it: yellow for south, white for north, red for east and black for west. At each of these points grew a sacred kapok (*ceiba*) tree the same color as the sector, where a bird of the same color is perched, and in the center of all stood the «great mother ceiba», or green ceiba, with its branches reaching up into the skies and its roots down into the underworld. The ceiba tree was thus the pivot of the world. This universe was vitalized by the movement of the Sun (*Kinich Ahau*) through the three different levels, since the Mayas believed that the Sun circled the Earth.

The universe was created for man to inhabit and had existed on several different occasions. It was cyclically put in order by the gods and destroyed by a catastrophe, only to be renewed yet again. The aim of this cy-

Left. Funeral mask in jade, shell and pyrite mosaic with a stone in its mouth symbolizing the immortal spirit. Burial 160 of Tikal. Classic period.

Above. Stone mosaic representing Kukulcán, the feathered serpent, on one of the walls of the Temple of the Warriors (Templo de los Guerreros) in Chichén Itzá. Postclassic period.

Masks of Chaac, god of Rain, covering the facade of the Codz Poop («Rolled Mat») Temple in Kabah, Yucatan. Classic Period.

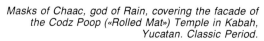

Censer from Mayapán, Yucatan, representing a priest of the god of Rain holding a small vessel in his right hand and a human heart in the left. Late Postclassic period.

cle of creation and destruction was the evolution of man, i.e. with every cosmic cycle man is perfected more and more until present-day man appears, who is made of maize dough. This man is a thinking being whose obligation is to worship and provide food for the gods so that they can continue to keep the universe alive. These religious beliefs formed the basis of the complex set of rites that Maya life revolved around. The main feature of ceremonies was nourishing the gods through various offerings. Since deities were invisible, intangible beings they fed on substances similar to themselves: the perfume of flowers and incense; the taste of dishes prepared for them and, in particular, the souls of men and animals, which lived in their hearts. So, the central aspects of ritual were offering one's own blood by «self-sacrifice» (blood was drawn from different parts of the body) and human sacrifice. The Mayas practiced several ways of human sacrifice: beheading, shooting full of arrows, drowning in the Sacred Cenote at Chichén Itzá, and cutting out the heart. This last practice seems to have been inherited from the peoples who migrated from the Central Plateau.

Self-sacrifice and human sacrifice were practiced in complex religious ceremonies related to calendar periods and included prayers, processions, dances, songs and dramatic performances. During the celebrations both priests and nobles consumed alcoholic drinks, which were held to be sacred because they prepared the spirit for its meeting with the gods.

There were also ceremonies for governors, family ceremonies connected with the life cycle, and rites for healing and divination, practiced by the magicians, in which they used hallucinogenic plants and mushrooms.

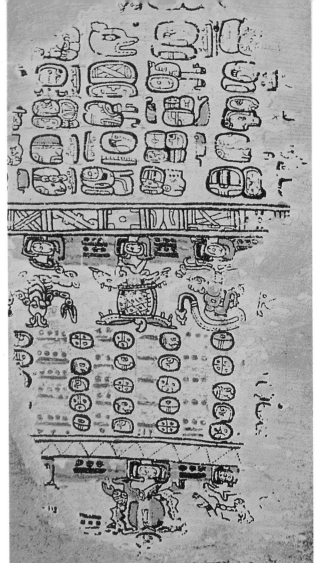

Above left. Page 6 of the Dresden Codex showing hieroglyphics, numerals and the figures of gods and priests.

Above right. Page 24 of the Paris Codex, with hieroglyphic inscriptions and animals with the Sun glyph coming out of their mouths. Above, a line of astral symbols.

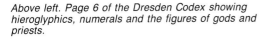

Facing page. Above. Page 34 of the Madrid Codex, with inscriptions, illustrations of offerings. In the upper part an astronomer extends his gaze to the stars.

SCIENTIFIC KNOWLEDGE

The Mayas' achievements in mathematics, the measurement of time, and astronomy are the most advanced of all ancient cultures. They came from a consciousness of flux, or «becoming», conceived as the movement of space, which seems to have been the essence of their culture. For the Mayas, the universe is not static, but in constant growth and expansion, which gives living beings a changing nature. But at the same time, since this movement is cyclical (days, seasons, etc.) it is regulated, and therefore given permanence and stability. As everything is repeated, including human history, the Mayas tried to keep some control over change by ordering and recording it. For this purpose they developed a complex system of writing, the most advanced in pre-Colombian America, and created a mathematical system with vigesimal numeration, the idea of zero and a value given to signs according to their position. Thanks

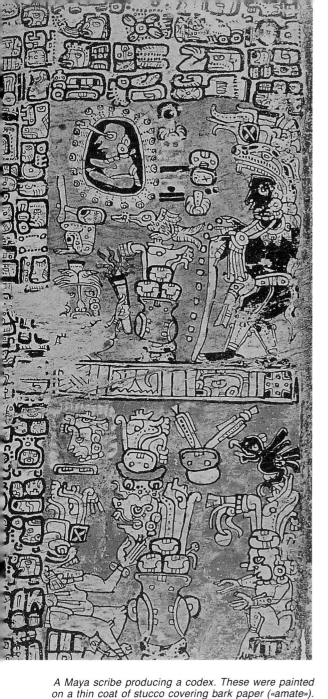

to this mathematical system and patient observation the Mayas arrived at a very accurate record of the cycles of the Sun, the Moon, Venus and other bodies. They were also able to develop a complete calendar system, basing their calculations on a «Period Beginning Date» (corresponding to August 13, 3113 B.C.). With all this as a foundation, the Mayas devoted themselves to calculating and recording dates using a complicated system called the Long Count, which uses several calendar systems.

WRITING AND MATHEMATICS

Maya writing and the numerical system originated in an area demarcated by Tres Zapotes, Veracruz (Olmec), Monte Alban, Oaxaca, and Chalchuapa, El Salvador. Numbers and some rudimentary glyphs appear on some Olmec monuments, but between 300 and 150 B.C. dates were already being recorded in the Long Count. The earliest date yet found is on Stele 2 from Chiapa de Corzo (Chiapas Highlands) and corresponds to 36 B.C., but the earliest known date from the Maya culture ap-

A Maya scribe producing a codex. These were painted on a thin coat of stucco covering bark paper («amate»).

pears on Stele 29 in Tikal, Guatemala (Central Area) and corresponds to 292 A.D.

The Maya system of writing numbers was the most sophisticated in all pre-Colombian America. It operated with dots (with a value of 1), bars (with a value of 5) and a stylized conch shell for zero. The numbers 1 to 20 could also be represented by human or animal head glyphs («head variants»), and for 1 to 13 there were also the «whole body variants». Dots and bars were usually arranged in vertical columns with the lowest number at the bottom; positional value meant that each numeral increased its value twenty times as it moved up the column, and the zero filled empty positions. This is why the Mayas called it «completing». For example, to write the number 20 a zero was placed at the bottom of the column (first position), and above (in second position) a dot. Using this system the Mayas could write any number whatsoever and carry out all mathematical operations. The Maya calculations we know of are all connected with the measurement of time, but they must have performed other mathematical operations.

Apart from numerals the system has hieroglyphs, or glyphs — stylized signs with variants. Each glyph is composed of a main element and several secondary ones, or affixes; together they form a cartouche; a series of cartouches produces a glyphic sentence, and several sentences together form a text. About 350 main signs have been identified, 350 affixes, and some 100 «portrait glyphs», mostly of deities.

The Mayas used to write on various materials. Codices are texts painted on long strips of beaten bark paper covered with a thin layer of stucco and folded like a screen. Only three codices survived destruction in Colonial times, now named as to where they are preserved: *Dresden*, *Madrid*, and *Paris*. They also left their texts sculpted, modeled or engraved on stone, stucco, clay, bone, shell and other materials. They embroidered them on clothes and painted them on the walls of ceremonial buildings and pottery.

In their texts the Mayas recorded their scientific knowledge, their myths and the history of the governing lineages (genealogies, biographies, military and political exploits and also the rites connected with their leaders).

Left. Stone slab from Yaxchilán, Chiapas, carved with hieroglyphs. Classic period.

Above. The name of the day 1 Ahau in a text about the governor Chan Bahlum of Palenque on a stone from Temple XIV. Classic Period.

A «whole body» glyph in a date of the Initial Series on the Palace Tablet, Palenque, showing the day 11 Ahau: a figure of the Sun god and a howler monkey inside a cartouche. Classic period.

Detail from an inscription about Chan Bahlum, governor of Palenque, on the tablet of Temple XIV. The upper right face is the Sun god G1, one of the main gods of the city. Classic period.

Head numbers, only from 0 to 19. These did not change their value according to position.

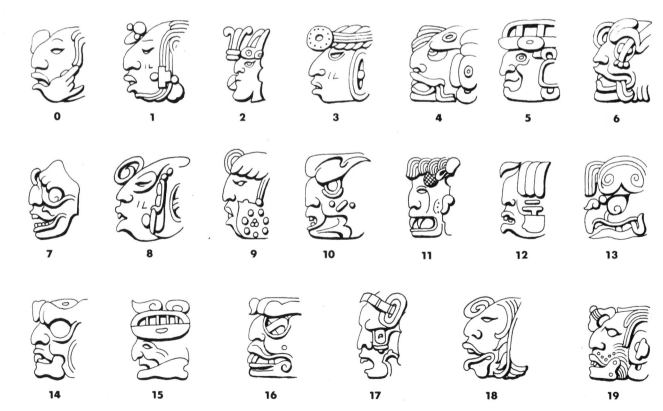

0   1   2   3   4   5   6

7   8   9   10   11   12   13

14   15   16   17   18   19

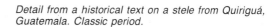
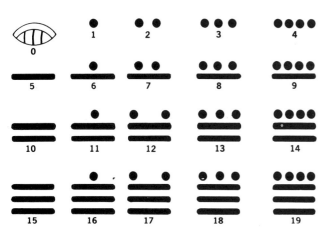

Dot and bar numerals from 0 to 19. Number 20 was written positionally by placing a zero in the first position and a dot in the second.

ASTRONOMY AND THE MEASUREMENT OF TIME

Thanks to their system of writing the Mayas were able to record their surprisingly advanced knowledge of astronomy. Firstly, they calculated the solar year as 365 days, almost the exact length of the Tropical Year, with an error of only 17.28 seconds; the lunar year with a deviation of 23 seconds and the cycle of Venus (584 days) with an error of one day in 6000 years. They also drew up tables for eclipses of the sun covering 33 years. They measured the cycles of other planets such as Mars, Jupiter and Saturn and the movements of various stars, such as the Pleiades (in Taurus), which they called *Tzab* (serpent's rattle), and the constellation of Geminis, or Ac (turtle).

These remarkable astronomical observations were made using only the most rudimentary instruments: a pole stuck vertically in the ground to measure the shadow cast by sun, and two crossed rods or threads to plot lines of sight drawn on reference points on the horizon so as to take a reading for the rising and setting of stars at different times of the year. They also constructed special buildings for making their observations, such as Group E in Uaxactún and the «Caracol» or Observatory at Chichén Itzá.

On the basis of their astronomical observations the Mayas created a solar calendar of 365 days divided into 18 months with 20 days each, plus five «extra» days. The Mayas of Yucatan called this Haab. Side by side with this calendar a lunar one (and others that have still not been studied in detail) governed both the life of the community and individual fate. This was a ritual calendar with 260 days, the *Tzolkin*, containing 20 signs and 13 numbers, which was used together with the Haab to date a particular day in any year (for example 4 *Ahau*, 8 *Cumhu*). So, each day was a new combination, and for the same one (4 *Ahau*, 8 *Cumhu*) to come around 18,980 days had to go by. In other words, the day was repeated once every 52 solar, or once every 73 ritual, years. This great cycle is known as the Calendar Round.

Altar Q at Copán, Honduras, showing a group of historical figures, perhaps astronomers meeting to make a correction to the calendar. 775 A.D. Classic period.

Preceding pages. The circular building called El Caracol at Chichen Itza. Dating from the Transitional period between the Classic and Post Classic, it was an astronomical observatory.

Sculpture of an astral god with large, snake-like eyes and a serpent in a figure 8 on his forehead. Copán, Honduras. Classic period.

Figurine from Jaina, Campeche, of a ball game player wearing a hip guard and other equipment. Classic period.

Ball game target from Chinkultic, Chiapas, with a player shooting a large ball from the hip. Hieroglyphs surround the scene. Classic period. 591 A.D.

The Mayas were using the Calendar Round for dates when the Spanish arrived, but in the Classic period they also invented the series of cycles on which the Long Count was based. With this they could pinpoint a date, starting from the «Period Beginning Date», both millions of years backward or forward. These periods range from one day (*Kin*) to an *Alautun*, or 64 million years. Maya knowledge of mathematics, astronomy and chronology can be regarded as coldly scientific from the conventional, Western point of view, but this does not mean that it was the opinion of its creators. Therefore it must be seen as a result of their own, special religious concept of the world and mankind. For the Mayas the universe was both the setting and the demonstration of sacred forces. So, since the stars are gods and mankind depends on them for existence, Maya astronomy can be considered as a way of becoming familiar with deities. The principal aim of it is to protect man from the forces that these supernatural beings unleash in the universe — which are sometimes hostile; to help him survive physically and to handle his fate, because by knowing what happened in the past, the future can be predicted. In other words science falls into the field of religion.

THE BALL GAME

The ball game was an important rite, as shown by the courts built in the ceremonial centers and in their reliefs. Notable examples are the ones in Copán, Honduras, and Chichén Itzá, Yucatan.
The symbolic and religious meaning of the game was the struggle between cosmic opposites that makes life

Ring target at the Ball Court of Uxmal, Yucatan. Classic period.

Ball Court of Chichén Itzá in the shape of «I» with several buildings attached to it. Post Classic.

Detail of the relief decorating the benches of the Ball Court at Chichén Itzá. It shows a ritual beheading performed by warrior-priests wearing outfit for the game. Post Classic.

possible. Some times it symbolizes the Sun's fight against the Moon; at others it is the conflict of the gods of the underworld (representing Death, Darkness and Evil) with the gods of heaven (the Sun and the Moon) that stand for Life, Light and Good. It is always linked to the stars, but also to sacred war. The ball game involved beheadings (perhaps prisoners of war) that were intended to increase fertility: the head symbolized the sun a or an ear of corn, represented in the game by the ball itself.

The ball game was played as a rite, and by imitating the struggle between opposing gods as well as the movement of the stars, ensured that these would be repeated so that the universe would continue to exist.

There are ball courts in almost all the cities and ceremonial centers in the Maya area. The structure consists of two rectangular platforms with either sloping or vertical walls that bounded the playing area. On these walls were the targets that had to be hit by the rubber ball; spectators occupied the top of the platforms. On some sites, e.g. Copán and Chichén Itzá the court also has platforms or walls at each end, like the courts on the Central Plateau.

The game was usually between two teams, each playing in one half of the court; the ball was thrown into play from the end of the court and had to be propelled with the hip. Only one throw was allowed, and a score was made either when the opposing team did not intercept the ball and it hit the wall at the end of the court or else if it hit the targets. Getting the ball through the stone rings earned a special score since it was so rarely accomplished.

Profile of governor Chan Bahlum on the tablet from Temple XIV at Palenque. He wears a headdress with a serpent head and long quetzal plumes hanging behind. Classic period.

Below. The quetzal, one of the birds sacred to the Mayas, lives in the Highlands. Its tail feathers were used to decorate the headdresses of the high lords.

HEADDRESSES AND COSTUME

Man has always tried to change his personal appearance for protection, magic or religious purposes, and for esthetic reasons, among others. Maya costume was not the same for all classes of society. Men usually wore a loincloth called *ex*; among the ordinary people these were plain, but among the upper classes they were richly embroidered and decorated with jade figurines and «trophy heads» that symbolized the wearer's warrior status. In addition to the loincloth they used to wear square cloak fastened over the shoulders. Peasant farmers wore only a loincloth, servants added a hip cloth and headdress, while the nobles wore rich, complex clothing. These last, as well as the *ex* wore short coats woven of cotton and decorated with feathers, coats, hip

Detail from a stele at Tikal, Guatemala. A serpent's head is tied to a man's calf. These heads were often used as heel guards on sandals. Classic period.

Facing page. Above left. Jaina figurine of a woman weaving on a backstrap loom. Classic period.

Facing page. Above right. Indian woman of San Andrés Larraínzar, Chiapas, weaving on a backstrap loom. One of the pre-Hispanic skills that has survived into the present.

cloths and long or short skirts, together with very decorative sandals and jewelry made of various materials (jade, jadeite, obsidian, shell or bone). Jewelry included hair ornaments, necklaces, earplugs, pectorals, lip plugs (inserted in the lower lip), nose plugs, bangles, anklets, bracelets and rings. The sandals, capes and skirts of governors were sometimes made of jaguar skin because the animal was associated with supreme power. Costume was completed by a wide variety of head ornaments: jade diadems, quetzal plumes, jeweled helmets «turbans», plaited bands, wide-brimmed hats, tiered masks of gods, snakes and jaguars, etc. These ornaments were combined with complicated hairstyles that meant letting the hair grow long. The hair on the top of the scalp was often cut to make stepped bangs over the forehead.

Merchants sported jewels, head coverings and — because their work meant covering long distances — fans. Warrior chiefs wore decorated capes and helmets with animal heads, perhaps to magically acquire ferocity. All women wore long skirts. In some regions they left their upper body bare, in others they covered themselves from the armpits down with a *huipil* (tunic) or *quechquémitl* (blouse), which were either plain or decorated with elaborate embroidery. Noblewomen wore short capes with tubular jade beads and feather fringes. All women seem to have worn necklaces and earplugs. Men and women of all the different classes painted their bodies, smearing themselves with resin scented with flowers. They also incrusted their teeth with precious stones and scarified their faces and bodies (except women's breasts), as can be seen on certain figures from Jaina. Other physical alterations were head deformation and crossed eyes, induced since childhood and possibly having a religious and magic meaning, such as identification with the sun god, who was portrayed as cross-eyed, and the belief that skull deformation would lead to visions or supernormal powers.

Metal ring with a bird's head from Playa del Carmen,
Quintana Roo. Post Classic period.

The Mayas did not work in gold but imported metal
jewelry from other regions, such as these gold earrings
found at Gumarcah, Guatemala.

Jade was the material most used by the Mayas for jewelry. Some beads discovered at Kohunlich, Quintana Roo.

Jade and shell necklace, an example of the jewelry worn by Maya nobles.

FAUNA

The Maya lands abound in big cats — jaguars, ocelots and pumas. The jaguar is perhaps the most important animal for the Mayas because of its strength, intelligence and ferocity. It was a religious symbol and is the animal most associated with men in power: the priest-governors in pre-Hispanic times and the shamans of today.

Other mammals in the Maya area that were either religious symbols or served as food are deer, monkeys (for example spider monkeys and howling monkeys with their impressive voices), tapirs, wild boars, armadillos, opossums, manatees, and bats.

Clay plate decorated with hunters disguised as deer to attract their prey. Classic period.

The deer hunt, an activity with a ritual meaning as the deer was a sacred animal, is shown on page 46 of the Madrid Codex.

Detail from Stele 20 at Tikàl, Guatemala. The jaguar was the companion of the governors, who identified themselves with it. Classic period.

There is a wide variety of fish, numberless insects, and birds with highly-prized feathers, such as macaws, toucans and cranes. The most valued birds were the enormous harpy eagle, over one meter tall, and the quetzal (trogon) which lives in the Highlands. This was one of the birds sacred to the Mayas, and its beautiful long tail feathers adorned the headdresses of high ranking lords.

Other common (and also sacred) animals in the area were reptiles such as turtles, iguanas, caimans and, above all, snakes. The most important of these are boas and snakes such as the tropical rattlesnake and the dreaded fer-de-lance and Mexican moccasin, whose neurotoxic and hemotoxic poisons kill within a few hours.

East Court and House C of the Palace at Palenque, Chiapas, where the priest-governors lived. Reliefs of nobles flank the stairs. On the left, the tower. Classic period.

DWELLINGS

Many of the great Maya archaeological sites now known are ceremonial centers, i.e. sites for worship, but many others (such as Tikal and Mayapán) were really urban centers with large concentrations of population. As well as religious and administrative buildings these contain markets and dwellings that are so different one from another that they can be supposed to be for members of the different social classes. They range from houses with many rooms and sometimes several stories (known as palaces), built of rough stonework and with vaulted ceilings, sited on platforms near religious and public buildings, to the remains of huts made of poles bound together and roofed with fan or cohune palm. Roofs were pitched (two slopes) or hip (four slopes) style,

either rectangular or semicircular, just like those of Maya huts today. These dwellings were located near cultivated areas. Cities followed a concentric pattern centered on the ceremonial buildings, with the housing of the lower classes on the outer edge. Near the main buildings there are ceremonial steam baths, shrines for family rites, grain stores and rainwater cisterns. In some of these buildings (the Palace of Palenque for instance) there were sanitary services such as latrines and drainage, and there may have been a system of channelling drinking water to the palaces, since they are located near rivers, lakes or wells («cenotes»).

Household furniture included benches, wooden frames for sleeping mats and poles for hanging up clothes. Palaces have benches fixed to the walls that perhaps served as beds, and stone rings on the sides of entrances for curtains.

Maya hut of today in Hopelchén, Yucatan, built of wood covered with stucco, with a sloping thatched roof. Peasant houses were the same in pre-Hispanic times.

Detail of a frieze on the Nunnery Quadrangle at Uxmal, Yucatan. It represents a Maya hut and above, a mask of the Rain god. Pre-Hispanic temples imitated huts with their vaults.

Above left. Female figurine from Jaina, Campeche, with another inside. It may allude to maternity or to the duality of the human spirit. Classic period.

Above right. Jaina figurine wearing a long skirt and cloak, with facial scarification. Classic period.

SCULPTURE, SEMI-PRECIOUS STONES, ENGRAVING, GOLD AND SILVER WORK

Clay Figurines

Though the Mayas used stone and stucco for their major sculptures, clay figurines also have an important place in their statuary. These were made from 1500 B.C. onward in several centers (Copán, Palenque, Jonuta, Kaminaljuyú, etc.), but the really outstanding ones are those from the island of Jaina, off the coast of Campeche (Mexico). These figurines, almost always around 25 cm. tall, are very realistic, expressing natural attitudes and movements. Some of them are of deities or animals, but the majority portray people belonging to all social classes, wearing complex costumes and engaged in different activities.

The figurines are either modeled or molded; they are

painted, with «Maya blue» used extensively in head-gear and clothing. Many of them are hollow, being used as whistles, rattles, ocarinas and flutes.

Classic and post-Classic sculpture

The cultural diversity of Maya speaking groups, as well as their political organization into independent states, led to different styles in their plastic arts. However, some common features can be distinguished in the sculpture of the Central and Northern areas.

Maya sculpture mainly takes the form of stelae and large blocks of stone, panels or slabs included in build-ings, stone mosaic facings, and works in clay, especial-ly large urns or incense burners. The sculpture of the Central area typically uses shapes inspired by nature or else human figures in both formal and expressive postures full of movement. Great men are portrayed,

Above left. Figure carrying a fan, as used by merchants. Jaina, Campeche. Classic period.

Above right. Jaina figurine of a naked man with a non-Maya face, probably a slave or prisoner of war. Classic period.

The movement captured in this Jaina figurine
led to its name «The Orator». Classic period.

with inscriptions about their personal history, myths
and the sciences.

In the Northern area there are hardly any stelae, and
sculpture is more in the nature of architectural decoration. It is typically in different geometric shapes symbolizing ideas and divine, human or natural beings. The
human figure is no longer the central element, attention being focused mainly on serpent-like gods in the
form of large masks made of stone mosaic on the friezes
and facades of buildings.

One of the central motifs of Maya sculpture in general
is the (usually) stylized serpent. It owes this high status
to the fact that the supreme god (*Itzamna*), the god of
rain (*Chaac*) and the god of the governors (*Bolon*

Dz'acab) are serpents. It also symbolizes the underworld
and death, and so represents the great contradictions
of the universe. *Itzamná* appears as a two-headed snake
or as a dragon, and he also figured on the «ceremonial
staff» that governors carried to signify that their power came from the supreme god. *Bolon D'zacab*, a god
in human form with snake-like features, is the deity who
is included in the portraits of governors over almost all
the Maya area. Sometimes he is shown as a humanoid
figure with one foot changed into a snake, as on the
«mannikin scepter» carried by high-ranking persons;
other times his head crowns a ceremonial staff, or he
appears as a child in the governor's arms. These gods
are not found at Chichen Itza, but the god that replaces

Maya lords wore imposing hats and coats, as shown by this figurine from Jaina. His coat is painted in classic «Maya blue». Classic period.

Figurine from Jaina in the typical Maya cross-legged position wearing another style of headgear painted in «Maya blue». Classic period.

Old man rising from a flower, a common motif in Maya figurines that illustrates man's ties to nature. Jaina, Campeche. Classic period.

Above left. Figurine of a dwarf. Maya religious beliefs held dwarfs and other abnormal beings sacred. Jaina, Campeche. Classic period.

Ocarina representing a mother goddess with her hands on her belly, with a large headdress and a two-headed serpent — symbol of the god of Heaven — behind her. Kaminaljuyú, Guatemala. Classic period.

Above left. Jaina figurine of a richly dressed governor. Classic period.

Above right. Clay urn from Teapa, Chiapas. It shows a man seated on a throne shaped like the face of a jaguar, wearing a headdress with a god's mask, surrounded by various symbols. Classic period.

them, *Kukulkán*, is a snake, now covered in feathers. As for the different styles in the Central area, the Peten region saw the beginnings of Maya plastic art that detached itself from the influence of Teotihuacán and the Izapa culture. The main cities are Uaxactún and Tikal, where the first stelae portraying the *Halach uinic* are found, in conjunction with altars. These stelae (carved only on the front with very delicate bas-relief) were erected when chronological periods finished, especially at the end of a Katun (20 years). This custom spread throughout the Central area and survived until the end of the Classic period as one of the most distinctive features of Maya civilization.

Other notable works in the Peten style are the carved

wooden lintels from temples. These also show the governor accompanied by the supreme god *Itzamná*.
Another Classic style developed in the region of the Motagua river and is called by the same name. The main sites here are Copan and Quirigua, where there are excellent sculptures dating mainly from the Late Classic period. The splendid stelae and altars are virtually sculptures in the round because of their pronounced high-relief. The stelae are carved on all four sides, with the leader always appearing on the front, heavily decorated and carrying the attributes of power but with an individualized face full of expression. The figure is shown full face, with the feet planted at an angle of 180 degrees (a ritual posture to be seen in all Maya cities); in his

Above left. Human figure in stucco on a pillar in the Palace at Palenque, Chiapas. Classic period.

Above right. Stucco head of Pacal, governor of Palenque, discovered under the sarcophagus containing his remains in the crypt of the Temple of the Inscriptions, Palenque. One of the masterpieces of Maya Art. Classic period.

Stele B at Copán portraying a governor in a ritual posture with all the symbols of his power. His enormous headdress in pierced high relief includes macaws, a sun animal. Classic period.

Left. This high relief on Stele C at Copán, Honduras, shows a governor. Over his chest he holds the ceremonial staff symbolizing the supreme god Itzamná. Classic period.

This rigid figure with a non-Maya face is a stele in Seibal, Guatemala.

arms he carries the ceremonial staff.

In front of the stelae there are altars depicting animals and gods, and in some cases there is a small underground chamber for offerings. This is evidence of ancestor worship, which survives among the Mayas of today.

Quiriguá was dependent on Copán and so the style of its sculpture is very similar. Some of the stelae on this site are very tall, for example stele E measures ten meters, but the most striking works are the large blocks of stone carved in high-relief with very stylized shapes,

usually animals. This has led to them being given the name «zoomorphic altars».

The Usumacinta style is found in the cities sited in the basin of this river: Piedras Negras, Yaxchilán and Bonampak. The bas-relief stelae, altars, thrones, lintels and other works of art at Piedras Negras are very skillfully carved. Striking features are the vigor shown in the human figures and the themes, which deal less with religion and more with court life and war. The main subject is again the *Halach uinic*, but here he appears in different scenes and rites, since some groups

Facing page. Above left. Stele at Quiriguá, Guatemala, a city dependent on Copán, Honduras, both in the Motagua style. The high governor carved in high relief. Classic period.

Facing page. Above right. Stele at Seibal, Guatemala, showing the Halach uinic, or supreme governor, with his face in profile. He carries a ceremonial staff and is surrounded by a hieroglyphic inscription. Classic period.

Facing page. Below left. Ahpo Hel presenting a figurine of the god Bolon D'zacab, patron of rulers, to her son, the governor Chan Bahlum.. Detail from the tablet in Temple XIV at Palenque. Classic period.

Facing page. Below right. The mother of the governor Chac Zutz', with a winged dragon on her head presents her son with a shield surmounted by an effigy of the god Bolon Dz'acab. Detail from the Tablet of the Slaves in Group IV at Palenque, Chiapas. Classic period.

Stone tablet from Jonuta, Tabasco with finely-worked relief of a figure wearing a phallic pectoral making an offering. Classic period.

illustrate his life. The most outstanding of these stelae is number 12, dating from 795 A.D., which is considered to be one of the masterpieces of Maya art because of its composition and technique. It shows two warriors presenting a group of prisoners to the chief, who is seated at the top of the scene.

In Yaxchilán, on the left bank of the Usumacinta, a large number of stelae and lintels were produced that bear mainly scenes of war and ceremonies. The *Halach uinicoob*, many of whom are called Bird-Jaguar and Shield-Jaguar, are almost always carrying a «mannikin scepter» and are shown either taking prisoners by the side of war leaders or else in the ceremonies for initiating chiefs, emerging from the jaws of a serpent (as on Lintel 25) or receiving the instruments for «self-sacrifice» or the sacred symbol for a shaman's equipment from the hands of a woman.

The city of Palenque in Chiapas created great sculptural art around the central theme of man that represents the highest degree of humanism reached by the Mayas in their plastic arts. The sculptors of Palenque worked mainly in reliefs; there are very few sculptures in the round, but among them are two masterpieces: the stucco heads found under the sarcophagus of the tomb in the Temple of the Inscriptions.

Here, governors were portrayed on stone slabs and in stucco moldings that covered the pillars of the main buildings. The *Halach uinic* is shown dressed very simply, accompanied by two or three secondary figures. In the stucco reliefs he is either carrying or receiving symbols of supreme power, such as ceremonial staffs, and on the stone slabs he is being offered diadems and shields. He is also shown in religious scenes, where he is the one making offerings to the principal gods.

«Chac Mool», a Toltec style
warrior sculpture for making
offerings. Chichén Itzá. Post
Classic period.

Wooden lintel carved with a
governor below a huge, two-
headed feathered serpent and
a bird with outstretched
wings. From Temple IV at
Tikal. Classic period.

Jade mosaic mask found on the cover of the sarcophagus in the Temple of the Inscriptions, Palenque. Classic period.

Lintel 43 in carved stone from Yaxchilán showing the Halach uinic carrying a ceremonial staff and receiving an offering from a woman. Classic period.

The human figure was sculpted and modeled with a high degree of technical perfection at Palenque; bodies are at the same time simple and elegant, with special attention paid to movement and the expression on faces and in the hands. Sculptors successfully aimed at showing the great lord in natural attitudes full of fluidity. The individualized features are remarkable, especially in the different stucco faces discovered in the city.

The most outstanding sculpture at Palenque, and in fact one of the masterpieces of Maya art in general, is the massive stone slab covering the sarcophagus in he Temple of the Inscriptions. It shows the buried chief, the great Pacal, reclining on symbols of death and the underworld, while above him rises a cross that represents the sky and the god of heaven, *Itzamná*. Among other things, this work symbolizes the idea that man, like corn, can expect resurrection after death.

Sculpture at Chichén Itzá is strongly influenced by the Central Plateau, in both subject matter and technique. Thus, the principal motifs are warriors, eagles and jaguars (symbolizing the semi-mystic military orders) and images of the god Quetzalcoatl whom the outsiders imposed on the Maya area, where he was known as *Kukulkán*.

Semi-precious stones and other materials

The Mayas produced hundreds of small objects in semi-precious stone such as jade and also in bone, shell and pyrites using only hard stone to cut them since they had no metal tools. These objects, whether in polished relief, engraved or carved in the round, were mainly costume decorations: jewelry, figurines for hanging on belts and items to include in headdresses. Motifs were geometric, animal, floral and humans either singly or in groups. Ritual objects were also produced in these materials, such as the excellent carvings in bone that have been found in tombs.

59

Jade pectoral showing a governor opposite the head of a serpent with a dwarf emerging from the open jaws. From Nebaj, Guatemala. Classic period.

Bone alligator with carved hieroglyphs.

Shell pectoral representing a person of high rank. Jaina.
Classic period.

Human figure carved in bone. Classic period.

Above left. Disk of turquoise and shell mosaic on wood showing four stylized serpents. Discovered in the substructure of El Castillo, Chichén Itzá. Classic period.

Above right. Classical Maya face in iron pyrites. Kohunlich, Quintana Roo. Classic period.

Repoussé gold disk showing human sacrifice. Above the scene, a warrior falls from the jaws of a serpent. From the Sacred Cenote of Chichén Itzá.

Jade pectoral in the shape of a high ranking chief holding his ceremonial staff. From Usumacinta. Classic period.

Gold and Silverware

The Mayas were not metalsmiths, but numerous metal objects were recovered from the Sacred Cenote in Chichén Itzá, including pieces made of gold, copper or tombac (an alloy of gold and copper), either hammered, molded or soldered. They include gold disks, disks of gold and precious stones, thin, rolled sheets, scepters, sandals, earplugs, pendants and bells as well as other things. Almost all these pieces come from outside the region (Panama, Costa Rica, the Mixtec area of Oaxaca and the Central Plateau) although some of them may have been produced at Chichén Itzá using metal from imported articles.

Scene from the great battle mural in Room 2 of the Temple of the Frescoes, Bonampak, Chiapas. Classic period. Copy in the National Museum of Anthropology, Mexico City.

Preceding pages. Palenque at its height; three nobles watch a funeral procession in front of the Temple of the Inscriptions.

Painting

Maya pictorial art is expressed mainly in murals and on pottery, but they also painted all their buildings, both inside and out, in bright colors. Unfortunately, most Maya painting has been lost.

They used both mineral and vegetable colors, which included red, ocher, yellow, black and the famous «Maya blue», produced by mixing indigo with certain clays that give it an extremely long life. Maya technique was to outline figures and then apply color either on a wet or dry surface (a *fresco* or *tempera*). In some cases they achieved three-dimensional effects with foreshortening and chiaroscuro. The oldest murals known are those at Tikal, which are influenced by Izapa style art. In Uaxactún the classic Maya themes are apparent: pictorial narratives with both ceremonial and historical content, full of naturalism and movement.

But the most splendid example of Maya painting, and one of the masterpieces of Mesoamerican art, are the frescoes of Bonampak, Chiapas, which date from the Late Classic era. These dramatic and technically perfect paintings show an event from Maya history — perhaps one of the many peasant revolts that took place at the end of the Late Classic period in the Maya area, together with the victory celebrations of the ruling class.

«Pellicer vessel» from Tabasco, with a court scene and hieroglyphic inscription. Classic period.

Right. Vessel from Altar de Sacrificios, Guatemala, discovered in Tomb 96. It depicts a shaman in an initiation rite involving snakes.

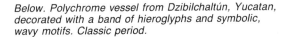

Below. Polychrome vessel from Dzibilchaltún, Yucatan, decorated with a band of hieroglyphs and symbolic, wavy motifs. Classic period.

Pottery

In all parts of the world the invention of pottery coincides with the beginnings of agriculture. The first vessels were of course practical — to keep and prepare food — and since food preparation was women's work, domestic pottery can also be supposed to have been their responsibility too. Domestic vessels are functional: undecorated or very simply painted cooking pots, plates and drinking vessels.

But not all clay vessels were for ordinary use: even at this time ceremonial vessels had started to be produced — incense burners, figurines of gods expressing religious ideas — that must have been the work of men, since women never participated actively in religious life. Ritual vessels were better made and had richer decoration. The potter's wheel was not known in Pre-Hispanic

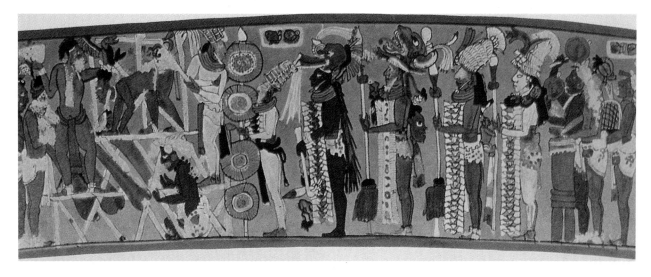

This scene on a vessel dating from the Classic period shows the preparations for a ritual sacrifice.

Right. A striking polychrome vessel on feet, decorated with subtle colors and an eye in relief. Classic period.

Polychrome vessel with a hieroglyphic text and a noble seated on a throne. Tikal. Classic period.

Mesoamerica, so all clay objects were hand-crafted, though the Mayas may have used a primitive wheel made up of two convex revolving plates. Pre-Hispanic Maya potters created a wide range of shapes and designs; their works in clay show their great creativity: no two vessels are alike, since they never reached the stage of mass production. However, they did have collective patterns or traditions that gave homogeneity to their work, and thanks to this, pottery has been a crucial element for archaeologists in establishing a chronology, since every culture and every epoch has its own, distinctive stamp.

The first pottery centers in the Maya area date from around 2000 B.C. These are Barra-Ocos (Pacific Coast) and Swasey-Bladen in northern Belize and central Yucatan. The pottery of these cultures is technically far advanced, which is evidence of a long-standing tradition.

Facing page. Polychrome vessel depicting a hunter disguised as a deer. San Agustín Acasahuastán, Guatemala. Classic period.

Facing page. polychrome vessel decorated with either a human-animal figure or a hunter disguised as a deer. Classic period.

Monochrome tripod vessel engraved with stylized serpents. Post Classic period.

Vessel decorated with a person of high rank.

Whistle vessel featuring an opossum. Kaminaljuyu, Guatemala.

Below left. Vessel incised with symbolical motifs.

Below right. Teotihuacan influenced vessel with applied jade mosaic and effigy lid. Burial 116 of Tikal. Classic period.

Vessel incised with hieroglyphics and a seated figure. Classic period.

Below. Puuc style vessel with incised geometrical decoration. Classic period.

Maya potters used the clay they had at hand in their different settlements. To remove grease from the clay and so make better pots they used powdered volcanic rock, sand, quartz and calcite, as well as some vegetable substances and powdered animal shells. Simple vessels have been discovered dating from the Classic period, and also ones resting on three supports, bowls with flared sides, dishes and plates. The pieces are covered with a layer of slip, and are monochrome — cream, black, orange red or gray. They were decorated with impressions of cloth, incisions, carving, clay applications and other methods before they were fired.

More elaborate shapes appear in the Protoclassic, such as plates standing on four, mammiform supports, and two-color decoration (red on yellow or orange) with geometric motifs (e.g. frets) or stylized animals.

Snail shaped vessel symbolizing birth with hieroglyphs in relief. Classic period.

Fine orange ware. A snail with an old man, possibly representing resurrection.

Polychrome funeral urn from El Quiché, Guatemala.

During the Early Classic Maya pottery, like other things, was strongly influenced by Teotihuacán, especially in the Southern area. There are tripod vessels with flat or «merlon» supports and rounded lids, and also pieces with molding on the base. Decoration was incised or painted either before or after firing, and the most common colors used are red and black on orange, though other colors were used, including some pastel shades. The designs continue to be geometric or stylized. In the Late Classic period pottery was rich and varied, and techniques were perfected. Among the wide range of shapes there are jugs, plates, vessels with handles, bowls with vertical or sloping sides, the characteristic tall, cylindrical vessels, incense burners and urns. Decoration is either incised, impressed, carved, appliqué or painted, and colors such as blue, purple, yellow and flesh are added to the ones used in the previous period. Designs now include geometric motifs, glyphs, animals (quetzals, eagles, bats, centipedes, jaguars), various plants, and human figures. «Court» scenes are common, where the *Halach uinic*, either seated on his throne or standing, receives offerings or presides over ceremonies. The paintings are very lifelike, full of dynamism and vigor. There are also scenes of rituals, including

Polychrome plate with hieroglyphs and a human figure adorned with feathers. Classic period.

Polychrome plate with a winged deity. Yucatan Peninsula. Classic period.

Polychrome plate with dancing figure circled with hieroglyphs. From a tomb in Structure A-1 in Uaxactun, Guatemala. Classic period.

the ceremony associated with deer hunting. Pottery was produced all over the Maya area, but the most important sites were Kaminaljuyu, Chama, Ratinlixul, Palenque, Teapa and Tapijulapa.

In the Early post-Classic the Maya area received influences from the Gulf Coast and the Central Plateau. The pottery known as fine orange ware was made, in the form of cylindrical vessels with bases, plates, bowls and tripod pots, decorated in black with geometric and animal designs, and pottery carved with volutes and flowers, or with modeled human or animal heads. Plumbate ware with its metallic sheen took the form of jugs, tripod bowls and animal-shaped vessels.

In the last phase of pre-Hispanic history, the Late pre-Classic, there is a decline in both the technique and style of pottery: the clay is coarse and badly fired, but there are many varied shapes designs such as tall cylindrical vessels, jugs with handles, vessels on pedestals, vessels with handles in the shape of animals, plates and bowls with supports in human or animal shapes, braziers on bell-shaped bases, with human figures, hollow human statues, incense burners, effigy vessels (with human or animal masks) and large urns sculpted in the round representing the priests of the different gods, or the gods themselves. Decoration is either monochrome or polychrome.

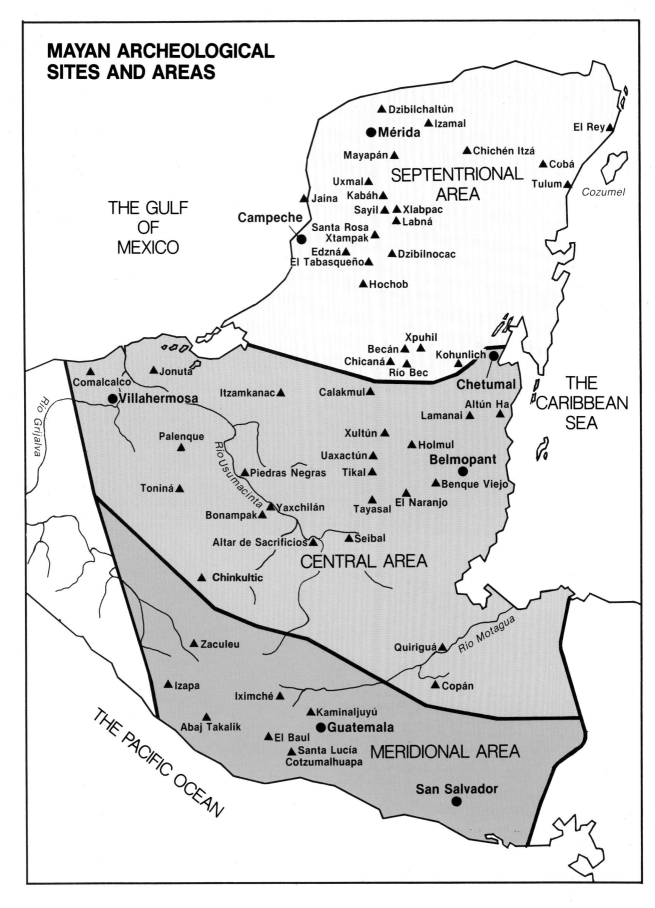

MAYAN ARCHEOLOGICAL SITES AND AREAS

THE GULF
OF
MEXICO

Campeche

▲ Dzibilchaltún
▲ Izamal
El Rey ▲
● Mérida
▲ Chichén Itzá
Mayapán ▲
▲ Cobá
SEPTENTRIONAL
AREA
Uxmal ▲
Tulum ▲
Cozumel
▲ Jaina
Kabáh ▲
Sayil ▲ ▲ Xlabpac
▲ Labná
Santa Rosa
Xtampak ▲
Edzná ▲
▲ Dzibilnocac
El Tabasqueño ▲
▲ Hochob

Xpuhil
Becán ▲ ▲
Chicaná ▲ ▲
Kohunlich ●
Río Bec ▲
Chetumal

THE
CARIBBEAN
SEA

▲ Jonutá
Comalcalco ▲
Itzamkanac ▲
Calakmul ▲
Altún Ha ▲
Lamanai ▲
● Villahermosa

Río Grijalva

Palenque ▲
Xultún ▲
Holmul ▲
Río Usumacinta
Uaxactún ▲
Belmopant
▲ Piedras Negras
Tikal ▲
●
Toniná ▲
▲ Benque Viejo
Tayasal ▲
El Naranjo ▲
Bonampak ▲ ▲ Yaxchilán
Altar de Sacrificios ▲ ▲ Seibal
CENTRAL AREA

▲ Chinkultic

▲ Zaculeu
Quiriguá ▲
Río Motagua

▲ Izapa
Iximché ▲
▲ Copán
▲ Kaminaljuyú
Abaj Takalik ▲
● Guatemala
▲ El Baul
▲ Santa Lucía
Cotzumalhuapa
MERIDIONAL AREA

● San Salvador

THE PACIFIC OCEAN

Structure E-VII-sub of Uaxactún, Guatemala, with large serpent masks at the sides of the staircases in the Izapa style. Pre Classic period.

Architecture

Fundamentally, Maya plastic art was guided not only by aesthetic sense but also by a deeply religious attitude towards life. This is why the most imposing Maya architecture is used in ceremonial constructions: squares, temples, ball courts, administrative buildings and houses for the governor-priests. But the Mayas were exceptionally creative, as shown by the wide variety of styles that developed in the different regions, though they all have typically Maya traits that distinguish them from the art of other Mesoamerican peoples. The main styles are generally known by the name of the region or site where they originated. These are, in the Central region Peten, Usumacinta, Motagua and Palenque; in the North-

ern area Río Bec, Chenes, Puuc, Maya-Toltec and Decadent. In the Southern area there are so many different sites that were constantly receiving external influences, especially from the Central Plateau (Teotihuacán, Toltec and Aztec), that it is more difficult to speak of Maya styles, but the most important cities here are Kaminaljuyu, Santa Lucia Cotzumalhuapa, Iximché and Zaculeu.

All the styles of the Central and Northern areas share certain general features, such as buildings of coarse masonry roofed with the Maya vault (false arch) and covered with stucco or polished stone (also with a thin layer of stucco), then finally painted in bright colors. The main structures are pyramidal bases of different dimensions topped by temples, and complexes of rooms

Temple of the Dolls, Dzibilchaltún, Yucatan; one of the largest Maya cities. This temple has a small central tower and some «windows»; the frieze is decorated with interlaced snakes. Classic period.

Right. Temple I, also known as the Temple of the Great Jaguar, Tikal, Guatemala. Built at different stages during the Classic period. The pyramid contains Burial 116. The temple has three rooms and is 45 meters high.

that are usually called «palaces», standing on stone platforms. Some of the pyramids are very high, as in Tikal for example, so as to rise above the rain forest and foster communications with the gods of the heavens. Also, the vaulted chambers have sloping or vertical walls on top to extend their height even further. These decorative, symbolic features are known as roof crests.

Cities and ceremonial centers were built on sites that, as well as their practical qualities had topographical features that were considered to be favorable for communicating with the gods; they were sites where divine forces were believed to concentrate or which were held especially suitable for invoking them. Buildings surround squares or courts and are adapted to the rise and fall of the terrain, but they are always aligned with the cardinal points or stars. It was also believed that constant ritual use made temples and ceremonial areas more and more sacred, and so when a new main temple was required it was built over the existing one so as not to lose the sacred forces that had accumulated in it. This explains why there are several layers to many buildings. The earliest sites in the Central area are those in the Peten, headed by Tikal, which inherited its style from Izapa. This was where the great monumental architecture

The South Acropolis, Temple I and the North Acropolis at Tikal. The great temples on this site tower over the high rain forest of the region. Classic period.

Right. The Great Plaza of Tikal, with Temple I, Temple II and the North Acropolis.

was created, together with the cultural patterns that would gradually spread throughout the Central area between 300 and 600 A.D.

The main cities in the Peten style are Tikal and Uaxactún, but there are many others, such as Holmul, Xultún, Naranjo, Calakmul, Xunantunich and Altun-Ha. All of these flourished during the Late Classic period, and Tikal was probably their capital, the largest center and the one with the highest pyramids (Temple IV rises to 70 meters, which is more than the Pyramid of the Sun at Teotihuacán).

The typical constructions of the Peten are temples made up of two or three parallel corridors with very thick

walls (up to seven meters) and very small interiors. This is because they had to support the weight of a massive roof crest decorated with stucco figures that rested on the rear wall of the temple (probably to approach closer to the gods and increase sanctity). Temples did not need to be more spacious because the population gathered in the squares at ceremonies. Architecture thus had a religious function, not a practical purpose. Palaces, such as those in the Central Acropolis of Tikal, have a great number of rooms and up to five stories.

Other typical features of Peten architecture are that pyramids have corners set back from one another, walls with recessed and protruding sections, and the profile of the stories of the pyramids is formed by a sloping wall, a narrow space and then a larger inclined wall. All this was meant to give movement to the great stone pile.

Cities in the Motagua styles are Copan, and Quirigua which was politically dependent on it. The architecture here is very different from the Peten style, since there are no tall pyramids (perhaps because it is not surrounded by towering rain forest), but rather complex groups such as the Acropolis containing pyramids, temples, courts and platforms, as well as a great square bordered by buildings where most of the site's imposing stelae stand.

Facing page. Above. Building at Altun Ha, Belize. The site belongs to the Central area and can be included in the Peten style. Classic period.

Facing page. Below. Temple of Río Bec, Campeche. This site gives its name to a style of art. The high towers at the sides of the temples are purely decorative and symbolic imitations of the pyramids of Tikal. Classic period.

Temple of Xpuhil, Campeche. in the Rio Bec style. Temples typically have decorative towers in an imitation of the Peten style. Classic period.

One of the most striking features at Copán is the «Hieroglyphic Staircase» on one of the pyramids, which has a total of almost 2,500 glyphs on its steps.
The temples are not covered with that thick layer of stucco found on other sites but with highly polished ashlar, with masks on the corners like the Puuc cities of the Yucatan Peninsula. Temple 22 is particularly interesting with its entrance surrounded with a stucco relief showing the three levels of the universe. Another remarkable structure at Copan is the Ball Court, which includes two earlier buildings. In one of these, «goals» were discovered with reliefs referring to the religious symbolism of the game, and on the structure to be seen today there are large stylized macaw heads set into the walls, a Sun symbol that affirms the astrological significance of the game.

Two main architectural styles developed in the vast Usumacinta region: Usumacinta and Palenque. The first includes sites such as Piedras Negras, Yaxchilán, Toniná, Bonampak, Chinkultic, Seibal, Altar de Sacrificios, Jonuta, and many more. The city of Palenque has a very similar style but includes elements that are so distinctive that it should be considered apart, together with the city of Comalcalco.

Usumacinta architecture was strongly influenced by the Peten style. In Piedras Negras there are pyramids with corners set back from one another, the sloping wall-narrow platform-sloping wall combination and massive

Great Plaza and Pyramid at Comalcalco, Tabasco. The site is notable mainly for its structures of sun-dried brick.

Facing page. Above. Stele D with the date 757 A.D. carved with a governor, and an altar in the shape of the fleshless head of the Earth Monster. Copán, Honduras. Classic period.

Facing page. Below. Ballcourt of Copán. Built in three stages, it has richly decorated targets showing the astral symbolism of the game. Classic period.

roof crests standing on the rear wall of temples. However, the architectural trend is less vertical, and the sanctuary more extended; also there are new elements such as porticoes with three bays. Yaxchilán has fewer Peten traits and is closer to the style of Palenque. Its roof crests are pierced and rest on the central wall separating the two corridors of the temple. Interiors are therefore wider, but sometimes the temples have only one corridor and the head of the vault could not bear the weight of the roof crest, so interiors were sacrificed by placing either columns or buttresses to support it. Once again, this is evidence that religious and aesthetic considerations were prime in Maya building. The most striking buildings are the beautiful Structure 33, erected under chief Bird-Jaguar IV, and Building 19, a complex of rooms called the Labyrinth.

Palenque shows a definite attempt to give more space and use to interiors, without losing the religious significance of buildings. Therefore corridors are wider and there are small T shaped openings in the walls for ventilation and light. Buildings usually have two parallel chambers covered by vaults and separated by a central wall; the outer parts are galleries with porticoes and the entrances leading to the other corridor have elegant arches, sometimes trilobate. Some buildings have oval or trilobate «windows» in the vault that give a feeling of spaciousness and provide better ventilation. On the wall separating the two corridors stands a pierced roof crest of two, slightly sloping walls, one on top of the other which used to be covered with stucco figures. The outside of the vaults forms a sloping frieze, framed by fine moldings, which is joined to the wall with a project-

Above. «Monster-Temple» at Chicaná, Campeche. The entire facade is sculpted as a large mask symbolizing a serpent, with its mouth forming the entrance to the temple. Classic period.

Facing page. Above. An imposing mountain setting for the Acropolis of Chinkultic, Chiapas, a site in the Usumacinta style. Classic period.

Facing page. Below. Pyramid at Xunantunich or Benque Viejo, Belize, a site in the Peten style. Classic period.

Left. El Rey, Cancún, Quintana Roo. Decadent style. Late post Classic.

Great Pyramid of Cobá, Quintana Roo, an important Classic city similar to those of the Central area, on the Yucatan Peninsula. The name, meaning «waters ruffled by the wind», is apt because there are several lakes in the region.

Facing page. Above. Temple of the Cross, Palenque, Chiapas. It takes its name from a stone tablet inside sculpted with a cross formed of two-headed serpents.

Facing page. Below left. The massive stone slab covering the sarcophagus in the Temple of the Inscriptions at Palenque. It is one of the masterpieces of Classic Maya sculpture and shows the life of Pacal, the governor buried in the crypt.

Facing page. Below right. This stucco head on the base of the Palace at Palenque is a fine example of Palenque craftsmen's art.

ing cornice. The architecture is very balanced, harmonious and light, avoiding great masses but nonetheless imposing and grandiose.

Among the main buildings at Palenque is The Palace, a complex of buildings surrounding courtyards that includes a curious tower with several stories. Because of its height this was used as a watchtower and perhaps as a sort of sundial but not, it appears, as an astronomical observatory.

The temples, built on different levels, are in the same style: two parallel corridors with a roof crest on the central wall. Some of them have a small sanctuary in the rear hall housing a carved stone slab.

The largest temple, built on the highest pyramid, is the Temple of the Inscriptions. This is one of the most famous temples in the whole of Mesoamerica because it was not simply the base for a temple like all the others, but a funeral monument. Inside there is a vaulted staircase leading down to the most magnificent burial chamber ever found in the Maya area.

Part of the Otulum that flows through the city of Palenque was covered over. Above, an example of a corbel vault formed with several courses of stone.

Gallery in the Palace at Palenque showing the Maya vault or false arch, covered with stucco, one of the most characteristic features of Maya architecture.

Preceding pages. View of the Palace with its curious tower, and the Temple of the Inscriptions, the two main buildings at Palenque, which developed its own artistic style.

Great Temple of Edzná, Campeche, in the old Puuc style. It is the only tiered pyramid with vaulted rooms on each level. On the top stands the temple with three galleries. Classic period.

Great Pyramid of Izamal, Yucatan, where Itzamna, the supreme god of the Maya pantheon, was worshiped.

Edifice 19 at Yaxchilan after reconstruction. At Yaxchilán, roof crests were built along the center of temples.

Edifice 19 at Yaxchilán, Chiapas, also known as «The Labyrinth» surrounded by forest, before reconstruction. Usumacinta style. Classic period.

Palenque's great art is largely due to an exceptional governor who lived in the 7th. century — Pacal or *Uox-oc Ahau* — for whom the Temple of the Inscriptions was built as a monument. His son *Chan Bahlum*, Jaguar Serpent, continued his father's work by ordering magnificent architectural and sculptural creations. The story of these two governors, as well as their past and later genealogy, is contained in the many texts that accompany the reliefs of the city.

While the Central area contains assortments of buildings planned only on the basis of astronomical observations, and high, pyramidal bases, these features are

Pyramid of Kohunlich, Quintana Roo, in the Río Bec region. Imposing masks decorate the different levels. Classic period.

Mask of the Sun god, Kinich Ahau, with large, squared eyes and serpent-like fangs in the corners of his mouth. Pyramid of Kohunlich. Classic period.

not found in the Northern area, save a few exceptions such as the Pyramid of the Magician at Uxmal. Bases are lower, groups more spacious and temples larger, covered with highly polished stone facing. Another element that becomes less important, and on some sites disappears entirely, is the roof crest. The favorite architectural decoration is the frieze, where there are various symbolical designs including masks of serpent gods with long noses, which seem to emerge from the upper jaw of the serpent.

The Río Bec, Chenes and Puuc styles are very similar. In the Río Bec style, which includes such cities as Xpu-

View of Uxmal, Yucatan, the most outstanding Puuc style city. It was at its height during the Classic period, and at end of this time was occupied by the Xiu from the Central Plateau.

Facing page. This building at Uxmal, which was part of a quadrangle, has been named The Dovecote because of the roof crest pierced by niches.

il, Chicaná and Becán as well as Río Bec itself, temples stand on low platforms but are accompanied by tall towers that resemble pyramidal bases and temples like those of Tikal and must have had deep religious meaning. The effect is a sort of symbolical setting. The exception to the rule is Kohunlich, belonging to the Río Bec region, where instead of decorative towers there is a pyramid with large masks of the sun god. In both this style and Chenes (which includes cities such as Hochob, Dzibilnocac and El Tabasqueno) temples are typically «monster-temples», i.e. the facade, made of stone mosaic, is an enormous mask with its mouth forming the entrance. The motif of the wide open jaws of serpents containing both men and gods is common in Mesoamerica. Open jaws seem to symbolize the caves

that are entrances to the underworld. At the same time, as they usually belong to serpents they also symbolize the initiation rites that are still practiced by some Mayance groups today. These involve a human being, swallowed by a huge snake and then either vomited or excreted, now possessing the supernatural powers of a shaman. To enter the underworld and return signified dying and then being reborn sanctified. This explains the serpent facades to temples, which perhaps only initiates entered or where these rites were performed.

The Chenes style does not include decorative towers, and shows influence from another style — Puuc — in the masks one above the other on the corners of temples.

The predominant style on the Yucatan Peninsula is

The Palace of the Governor at Uxmal was the seat of government, as shown by the double jaguar throne in front.

Facing page. Above. The Nunnery Quadrangle at Uxmal was given this name in Colonial times because of its many cell-like rooms.

Facing page. Below. The Pyramid of the Magician at Uxmal has an elliptical base.

Puuc, and the most important city Uxmal, which flourished in the Late Classic period. Buildings in the Puuc style are low, except for certain temples that stand on fairly high pyramidal bases. Generally, four buildings surround almost square courts, like the Quadrangle of the Nuns and the Dovecote at Uxmal. Some buildings stand on large stone platforms, like the magnificent Governor's Palace, where the Mayas achieved what the Greeks called the «Golden Section».

To the columns of masks on the corners of temples, friezes and facades are added frets, latticework, pillars, beading, toothed lozenges, serpent heads and peasant huts. All this is done in stone mosaic that was then covered with a thin coat of stucco and painted. Temple friezes are vertical, and larger than those in the Cen-

tral area. The cities of Edzná, Labná, Kabáh, Sayil, Xlabpak and Chichén Itzá also belong to the Puuc style although the last one is located outside the region.

Around 1000 A.D. the Maya area was invaded by groups from the Central Plateau who brought with them Toltec culture. Among them were the Itzas, who settled at Chichén Itzá. According to native texts dating from Colonial times, the Itzas had lived in Chichen Itza previously, then had migrated to Chakamputún (now Champotón) on the Laguna de Terminos in Campeche. Whatever the truth, their arrival caused a great cultural change in the city, and a new area was built combining Maya and Toltec architectural styles.

The first new structure to appear in the Classic city was the circular building known as The Caracol because of

Above left. The Nahua invaders placed a feathered serpent on the frieze of the Nunnery Quadrangle at Uxmal as a sign of their presence.

Above right. The Palace of the Governor at Uxmal is one of the masterpieces of Maya architecture in which the «Golden Section» of the Greeks was achieved. Classic period.

Facing page. Below. Standing on the same platform as the Palace of the Governor is a small temple called the House of the Turtles because its frieze of small columns is decorated with small, carved turtles.

Part of the East Building of the Nunnery Quadrangle at Uxmal. On the lattice decoration of the frieze, trapeziums of seven, two-headed serpents alternate with tiered masks of the god of Heaven.

Chaac the god of Rain as a «descending god», between two large serpents on the frieze of the second story of the Palace at Sayil.

The Palace at Sayil, a city in the Puuc region, Yucatan, dating from the Classic period. It has three, tiered stories with many rooms. The main decorative features are the differently shaped columns.

Temple in the city of Kabáh, Yucatan, in the Puuc region, known as Codz Poop («rolled mat») because of the large masks resembling scrolled noses that form the stairs up to the temple. Classic period.

Below. The Codz Poop at Kabáh is completely covered with masks of the god of Rain, decorating the base platform, the walls and the frieze of the temple. Classic period.

Standing in isolation in the Puuc city of Labná, Yucatan, is one of the finest arches in all Maya architecture. One of the friezes is decorated with frets and the other with Maya huts. Classic period.

the spiral staircase inside. It is considered as a transitional work, and was built for astronomical observations.

One or several of the chieftains who led the waves of immigrants was *Kukulcán* (the Maya version of the name Quetzalcoatl). He was most probably a priest of the god with the same name, who imposed his cult on Chichén Itzá, which would determine future architecture. The main structure is the pyramid known as El Castillo (The Castle), topped by a temple in which the

Maya vault still appears, but the roof crest has been replaced by decoration representing sections of conch shells, which are symbols of Quetzalcóatl. The building covers an earlier one, in the same style, whose temple contains a remarkable red jaguar inset with jade disks.

«New» Chichén Itzá also contains the Temple of the Warriors, the Platform of Venus, the Platform of Eagles and Jaguars, the Tzompantli («Wall of Skulls») and the Ball Court, which is one of the largest in Mesoameri-

The governors of Labná lived in a magnificent two-story palace decorated with frets, columnettes, masks and other Puuc features. Classic period.

A remarkable sculpture on the Palace at Labná is a serpent mask whose open jaws contain a human face. It symbolizes the sanctification of the governor through a serpent.

Left. Temple called the Watchtower, Labná, with a roof crest built on the front wall. Classic period.

Below. Ruins of Mayapán, Yucatan. Post Classic period, Decadent style. The buildings of Mayapan are poor copies of those at Chichen Itza.

Facing page. Above. The Great Pyramid of Tulum, known as The Castle, on the Caribbean coast. This city stands in a remarkable location.

Facing page. Below. Aerial view of Tulum, Quintana Roo, the most important site dating from the Decadent phase of the post Classic period. The city was walled because of the constant wars between different Maya groups.

Facing page. Above. A watchtower perched on a cliff overlooking the Caribbean at Tulum. Classic period.

Facing page. Below. The Castle at Tulum, which the Spanish compared to the Giralda of Seville when they saw it from out at sea, is the largest temple in the city. Decadent style.

Front of the temple of the Warriors at Chichén Itzá, Yucatan. Post Classic period, Maya-Toltec style. Behind the statue of a Toltec warrior (a Chac Mool) are the two serpent shaped columns that originally framed the entrance. The roof of the temple has disappeared.

ca. Maya-Toltec style is characterized by the use of pillars and columns, flat roofs combined with vaults, sloping and vertical walls decorated with eagles and jaguars devouring hearts (symbols of the semi-mystic Toltec warrior orders of «Eagle Knights» and «Jaguar Knights»), pillars with reliefs of warriors carrying Toltec weapons and wearing butterfly shaped pectorals (meaning that they were initiates), serpent columns with the head at the base and the rattle as capital, and sculptures of reclining warriors («Chac Mool»).

The I shaped Ball Court has several temples attached to it and some striking reliefs that show the ceremony of beheading warrior-players.
Chichén Itzá lost its dominance around 1200 A.D. to be replaced by Mayapán. This city, Tulum on the Quintana Roo coast and many others dating from the Late pre-Classic were built in a style known as Decadent: for example, the architecture of Mayapán is a coarse imitation of Chichén Itzá. This is because interest was focused on utilitarian and state interests, and on

Above. The Thousand Columns Group at Chichén Itzá originally supported a flat roof, as in all Toltec buildings. Post Classic period. Maya-Toltec style.

Right. Sculpted columns at the entrance to the Jaguar Temple Annex at Chichén Itzá. Inside this temple there are magnificent reliefs of ritual scenes. Post Classic period.

Facing page. Above. The Thousand Columns Group and Temple of the Warriors at Chichén Itzá — two of the main structures built by the Toltec invaders. They combine Maya and Toltec styles.

Facing page. Below. Relief of eagles and jaguars devouring hearts on the Temple of the Warriors at Chichén Itzá. This symbolizes the two military orders of «Eagle Knights» and «Jaguar Knights» that conquered the city around 1000 A.D.

Preceding pages. Aerial view of the Great Plaza in the Toltec part of Chichén Itzá. Left, the Castle; foreground, the Temple of the Warriors and the Thousand Columns Group; rear, the Ballcourt.

The Temple of the Jaguars and its Annex back onto the Ballcourt at Chichén Itzá.

Facing page. Above. The Classic city of Chichén Itzá is in the Puuc style. Among the buildings of this period are the Church and the richly decorated Nunnery Annex.

Faging page. Below. Arch of the Temple of the Lintels (Templo de los Tableros) and in the background Caracol, in the style of Puuc area of Chichén Itzá. Classic period.

militarism. On the Quintana Roo coast, cities were protected by defense walls, like at Tulum. In this city, the Decadent style is apparent in coarsely styled buildings covered with thick layers of stucco to cover up defects, small buildings with walls sloping outwards from the base, and misaligned friezes. At the same time there are frescoes and friezes showing the «descending god» (i.e. head downward) symbolizing either rain or else the setting sun.

One of the Toltec buildings at Chichén Itzá is the Tzompantli or «place of skulls». This platform, where the heads of ritually beheaded victims were displayed, was decorated with skulls. Post Classic period.

Facing page. A group of Tzeltal Mayas of Tenejapa, Chiapas. Most of the 28 Maya groups have survived through Colonial times and the many political changes that have occurred in their lands.

CHRONOLOGICAL TABLE OF THE MAYA CIVILIZATION

DATE	PERIOD	CULTURAL ELEMENTS
1500 A.D. 1250 A.D.	LATE POST CLASSIC	Decadence in art; increase in trade and militarism in the Northern area. Height of the Quiché Empire.
1000 A.D.	EARLY POST CLASSIC	Arrival of Toltec Groups. Culture flourishes in the Northern and Southern areas
900 A.D.	TRANSITIONAL	Nahua influences in the Southern area; cultural collapse of the Central area; Nahua influences in the Northern area.
600 A.D.	LATE CLASSIC	Flourishing of ceremonial centers and cities. Development of arts, science and the recording of history.
300 A.D.	EARLY CLASSIC	Development of agriculture, writing and science. Influences from Teotihuacán.
150 A.D.	PROTOCLASSIC	Integration of Izapa culture into Maya culture.
300 B.C.	UPPER PRE-CLASSIC	Differentiation of Maya culture. Beginning of hieroglyphic writing. Olmec influences. Height of Izapa culture.
800 B.C.	MIDDLE PRE-CLASSIC	Great progress in the cultivation of maize. Villages.
1500 B.C.	LOWER PRE-CLASSIC	Economy based on food collecting, hunting and fishing. Beginning of maize growing.

THE MAYAS OF TODAY

During the Colonial period ethnic communities were isolated by the confines imposed by the Spanish authorities, unlike in pre-Hispanic times. This led to an even greater differentiation of Maya groups because although they continued to speak their own language they lost contact with other groups. As a result the Maya area includes a wide variety of social, economic and general culture patterns but with common traits that identify them as Maya.

Most groups depend on agriculture for their livelihood, especially corn growing, following the pre-Hispanic slash-and-burn system and fallow land. Some groups also have a market economy based on specialized handicrafts. They own almost all the land they live on, but this is not usually best quality. Because of the agricultural system settlements are scattered: there is one village with a church, a court, shops and a few houses, but most people live outside these nucleuses in «parajes», which are small groups of huts generally inhabited by an extended family whose members work

Facing page. Maya woman with her daughter. They have the characteristic features included in all pre-Hispanic Maya works.

together. Several «parajes» together make up a Municipality, with the village as the political, religious and economic center.

The political and religious structure combines pre-Hispanic and Colonial elements in a complex system of posts that includes constables, chiefs, etc. responsible for protecting and serving the community and at the same time for doing homage to saints. Among the most respected figures are the different types of shamans. They are basically healers and prophesiers, but some of them — the most powerful — practice sorcery. This means, according to them, that they can turn themselves into animals, lightning, thunderbolts and comets and can also cause different sicknesses and even death.

New religious forms have been created. Some of them combine pre-Hispanic and modern ideas; others are the result of a syncretism that evolved in Colonial times. Thus the Mayas venerate their old gods of nature and their ancestors in fields, caves and mountains that are the main sacred sites, and at the same time worship saints in church, although in very different ways than prescribed by Catholic ritual, and often without Christian priests.

Intimacy with the natural world, so important in pre-Hispanic times, has not been lost: the Mayas still feel in close touch with nature, among other ways through the conviction that a part of their soul lives inside a jungle animal, the «animal of destiny», to which every man is connected from birth to death. According to some groups the other animal self of every human lives on a sacred mountain near the village, protected and fed by deified ancestors and by the animal companions of the most important men in the community, which are jaguars, pumas and coyotes. This is just one of the many pre-Hispanic beliefs that survive.

So, the Mayas must not be seen as a mysterious people that suddenly disappeared, as is often claimed. The builders of such great cities as Palenque and Chichen Itza did not originate in Asia, nor were they beings from outer space; they were the ancestors of the Mayas that continue to speak their own languages and worship their gods on their original lands; a people that, as if fed by an underground current, preserve their ancestral heritage.

The Lacandons, Maya groups originally from the
Yucatan Peninsula, still live in the rain forest of
Chiapas.

Facing page. Above. A Tzotzil family in front of their
hut. San Miguel Mitotik, Chiapas.

Facing page. Below. The ceremony of Balché, a sacred
drink dating from pre-Hispanic times, is still performed
among the Lacandons of Lacanja, Chiapas.

Offerings to a stone idol in Chichicastenango,
Guatemala shows that pre-Hispanic rites are still
practiced.

Carnival is one of the most important religious festivities of the Mayas. Participants usually wear masks representing jaguars or other beings, such as here in Tenosique, Chiapas.

One of the figures included in the carnival of Tenejapa, Chiapas, is the «Torito» (Little Bull). The Mayas of today still preserve many of their ancient traditions in religious festivities.

GLOSSARY

Ac: «Turtle» - the Maya name for the constellation Geminis.

Ah chembal uinicoob: «inferior men» i.e. peasants.

Ah Puch: «The Fleshless One», God of Death.

Ahau: One of the days of the Maya ritual calender.

Ahau Can: «Lord Serpent» or high priest.

Ahpo Hel: The Lady of Palenque, mother of the governor Chan Bahlum.

Alauntun: A period of 64 million years.

Amate: Name given to several different trees whose bark is used to make paper, also called amate.

Almehenoob: Nobles, persons of noble lineage; the highest social class.

Batabes: Title given to the governors of cities dependent on a larger or more important one.

Balon Dz'acab: God of the chiefs, with human form and serpent features.

Cakchiquel: A Maya language spoken in Guatemala.

Codz Poop: The largest building at Kabah. The name means «Rolled Mat».

Cumhu: One of the months of the Maya calendar.

Chaac: Maya god of Rain.

Chac Mool: Semi-reclining sculpted figure, with knees bent and head turned to one side.

Chac Mumul Ain: The Yucatec Maya name for the Earth, meaning «Great Muddy Crocodile».

Chac Zutz': Name of one of the governors of Palenque.

Chan Bahlum: «Jaguar-Serpent», governor of Palenque who succeeded his father, Pacal.

Chontal: A Maya language, also called Chontal of Tabasco because it is spoken in this state.

Chuj: A Maya language spoken in Chiapas and Guatemala.

Dzonot: «Cenote» (well) in Maya.

Ex: Loincloth worn by Maya men.

Haab: The Maya solar calendar of 365 days, divided into 18 months with 20 days each, and five «extra» days.

Halach uinic: «True man» or chief governor.

Halach uinicoob: «Supreme governors or 'True men'».

Huipil: Long, native tunic worn by women. Rectangular in shape and generally made of three lengths of cloth stitched together.

Itzamná: «The dragon», supreme deity in the Maya pantheon, representing the heavens.

Ixchebel Yax: Patroness of the art of embroidery and according to Maya mythology the daughter of Ixchel.

Ixchel: Goddess of the Moon, weaving, childbirth and medicines.

Kanjobal: Maya language spoken in Guatemala.

Katunes: Periods of twenty years.

Kekchi: Maya language spoken in Guatemala and Belize.

Kin: Day.

Kinich Ahau: God of the Sun.

Kisin: «The Decomposed», one of the names given to the god of Death.

Kukulkan: The Maya name for Quetzalcoatl.

Lacandon: Maya language spoken in the State of Chiapas.

Nohok Ek: The god representing the planet Venus.

Pacal: Name of the governor buried in the sarcophagus in the Temple of the Inscriptions at Palenque.

Pentacoob: Slaves. These were not numerous and were prisoners of war, criminals, orphans and children of slaves.

Pokomam: Maya language spoken in Guatemala.

Pokomchi: Maya language spoken in Guatemala.

Popol Vuh: The sacred book of the Quiche Mayas; also called the Book of Council.

Puuc: Maya term meaning mountain chain; also the name given to an architectural style of the region.

Quechquemitl: Native garment worn by Maya women: a square of material embroidered and decorated, with an opening for the head in the center.

Quiché: Maya language spoken in Chiapas and Guatemala.

Tlaloc: The Teotihuacan god of Rain and Thunder.

Tzab: Maya name for the Pleiades, meaning «serpent rattle».

Tzeltal: Maya language spoken in Chiapas.

Tzolkin: The Maya ritual calendar of 260 days, made up of 20 signs and 12 numerals that are combined to name days.

Tzompantli: «Place» or «Wall of Skulls». A platform where the heads of those ritually decapitated were exhibited.

Tzotzil: Maya language spoken in the State of Chiapas.

Uoxoc Ahau: One of the names given to Pacal (q.v.).

THE MAYAS

Project and editorial conception: Casa Editrice Bonechi
Publication Manager: Monica Bonechi
Cover and layout: Sonia Gottardo
Editing: Simonetta Giorgi

© Copyright by Casa Editrice Bonechi,
Via Cairoli 18b
50131 Firenze, Italia
Tel. +39 55 576841 - Fax +39 55 5000766
E-mail: bonechi@bonechi.it - Internet: www.bonechi.it

ISBN 88-8029-020-7

THE MAYAS

Project and editorial conception: Monclem Ediciones
Publication Manager: Concepción Cadena
Cover and layout: Angel Escobar
Editing: Angel Escobar
Translated by David Castledine

© Copyright by Monclem Ediciones, S.A. de C.V.
Leibnitz 31
Col. Anzures
11590 México, D.F.-México
Tel. 520 81 67 - Fax 202 88 14

ISBN 968-6434-26-7

Printed in Italy by
Centro Stampa Editoriale Bonechi

Distribution by
Monclem Ediciones S.A. de C.V.
Leibnitz 31
Col. Anzures
11590 México, D.F.-México
Tel. 545 77 42
Fax 203 46 57

* * *

The Author:
*Dr. Mercedes de la Garza is an expert on the Mayas and Na-
huas. She was Director of the Center for Maya Studies in the
National University of Mexico for several years.*

ACKNOWLEDGEMENTS

PHOTOGRAPHS:

Enrique Franco Torrijos
*Pages 5; 6; 8; 9 above; 10; 12 above and below; 13 above and
below, 15 above; 16 above left and right; 17 left; 19; 20 above;
22; 23 above and below; 24 above left and right; 28, 29 below; 31; 32-33; 34 above and below; 35 left; 36-37; 40; 41
above left; 41 above left; 41 below left and right; 42 above;
43 below; 45 above and below; 50 right; 51 above right and
below; 52 left; 53 left; 54; 55 above; 56 above left and right;
56 below right; 59 right; 60 above; 61 right; 62 above right;
67; 69; 71; 72 above; 74 above; 74 below right; 77; 79; 81;
82; 84; 84-85; 86 above and below; 87; 88; 89 above and below; 90 above and below; 91 above and below; 92; 94-95; 96
below; 97 above and below; 98 above; 99 above and below;
100; 101; 102; 103 below; 104 above; 104-105 above; 106 above
and below; 107 below; 108; 109 above and below; 110 above;
111 below; 112 above; 114-115; 116 above and below; 177
above and below; 119 above and below; 122; 123; 124 above;
125 below.*

Irmgard Groth
*Pages 4; 9 below; 11; 15 below; 17 right; 18, 24 below; 25;
29 above; 30; 39 above; 43 above; 46 left and right; 47 left
and right; 48; 49; 50 left; 51 above left; 52 right; 53 right;
56 below left; 57; 58 above and below; 59 left; 60 below; 61
let; 63; 68 above and below; 70 below; 74 below left; 75 above
and below; 76 above and below; 78 above and below 93 above;
93 below left and right; 96 above; 98 below; 120; 124 below;
125 above.*

Walter Reuter
Pages 38; 103 above; 104 below; 112 below; 113.

Ruth Lechuga
Pages 41 above right; 121; 126 above and below.

Armando Salas Portugal
Page 42 below.

Guillermo Aldana
Page 110 below.

Bonechi Archives
*Pages 21 above; 20 below; 35 right; 36 above; 44; 55 below;
62 above left; 66 above and below; 83; 105 below; 107 above;
11 above; 118.*

Monclem Archives
Pages 14; 16 below; 26 left and right; 27 above; 70 above.

DRAWINGS:

Heraclio Ramirez
Pages 7; 27; 39; 64-65.

MUSEUMS:
*Museo Nacional de Antropologia, Mexico City.
Museo de la Aurora, Guatemala City.
Museo Regional de Villahermosa, Tabasco, Mexico.
Museo Regional de Merida, Yucatan, Mexico.*